The 40-Day Challenge

A companion workbook to
"Journaling with Jesus: How to draw closer to God"

CAROL ROUND

THE 40-DAY CHALLENGE:
A companion workbook to Journaling with Jesus—How to draw closer to God

Copyright © 2012 by Carol Round

Unless otherwise indicated, all scripture quotations cited in this book are from *The Holy Bible, New International Version, NIV* Copyright ©1973, 1978, 1984, 2011 by Biblica, Inc.

Cover design by Carol Round

This workbook can be ordered through www.amazon.com or by contacting the author at **www.carolaround.com**.

Any people depicted in stock imagery provided by iStockphoto are models and such images are being used for illustrative purposes only.

Certain stock imagery © iStockphoto.

ISBN:0615691714
ISBN:9780615691718

Library of Congress Control Number:

Printed in the United States of America

Passionate Purpose Publishing

Acknowledgements

Thank you, Lord Jesus, for not giving up on me, a sinner. When I cried out for direction in October 2001, You answered my pleas. I once was lost but now I'm found, was blind, but now I see.

Thank You for covering me in Your *Amazing Grace.*

Introduction

Are you as close to God as you want to be? If not, why?

God has created us to be in relationship with Him. Inside each of us is a space that can only be filled by Him. For years—over 40 decades—I tried to fill that God-shaped hole with other things: people's approval, a busy life, unhealthy relationships and material things. I was 47 when I cried out to God for direction in my life. My 28-year marriage had ended, my children were grown and I was lost.

Since October 2001, I have been on a journey to know Him better, to grow into the woman He created me to be and to follow the path He has laid out for me. Do I always get it right? No. Am I perfect? Not hardly. However, He is and His perfect plan is the one I seek.

Through keeping a daily prayer journal, I have discovered the following:

- God loves me unconditionally.
- He forgives me and asks me to forgive myself for past mistakes.
- Although He loves me as I am, He wants to do an extreme makeover on me—from the inside out.
- To grow spiritually, you will experience pain. I have learned that we grow in the valleys and not on the mountaintops.
- When I am weak, He is strong.
- He will never leave me nor forsake me.
- I can trust Him with my heart. He will lead me on the right path.
- When you surrender your life to Him, the real adventure begins.

I could continue with my list but the benefits of prayer journaling are ones you will experience for yourself when you take the challenge to try it for 40 days. Why 40 days? Because, according to the Bible, God made major changes and transformations during periods of 40 days.

- It rained for 40 days and 40 nights when God wanted to cleanse the world and start over. (*Genesis 7:12 NIV*)
- Noah waited another 40 days after it rained before he opened a window in the Ark." (*Genesis 8:6 NIV*)
- Moses was on the mountain with God for 40 days (twice). (*Exodus 24:18 NIV*) (*Exodus 34:28 NIV*) (*Deuteronomy* 10:10 NIV)
- The Israelites spent 40 years in the wilderness, one year for each day they explored the Promised Land. (*Exodus 16:35 NIV*)
- Jonah warned the City of Nineveh they had 40 days until God would overthrow the city. The people repented in those 40 days and God spared the city. (*Jonah 3:4 NIV*)
- Jesus fasted for 40 days in the wilderness. (*Matthew 4:1-2 NIV*)

I pray that you are hungry for more of God in your life. Won't you join me for the next 40 days and through prayer journaling let Jesus change your life?

Day 1
Get Closer to God

"Be still and know that I am God"— Psalm 46:10 (NIV).

Are you as close to God as you want to be? Spending time with Your Heavenly Father is the best relationship you can ever develop. When you spend time getting to know Him, the rest of your relationships will improve. Never let a day pass without spending time with Your Creator. This simple practice can change your life forever.

Dear Father,

I want to know you better, Father. Please teach me what I need to learn in order to draw closer to You.

With love,

Me

_____
_____
_____
_____
_____
_____
_____
_____
_____
_____
_____
_____
_____
_____
_____
_____
_____
_____
_____
_____
_____
_____
_____
_____
_____
_____
_____

Faith Step: Choose to put God above all else each day by getting up earlier, if necessary, to read the Bible and journal your prayers to Him. What would you like to say to Him today?

Day 2
Relying on God's Strength

"Brothers and sisters, think of what you were when you were called. Not many of you were wise by human standards...God chose the weak things of the world to shame the strong"— 1 Corinthians 1:26–27 (NIV).

When I was younger, I relied on my parents. Later on in life, I relied on others until they proved untrustworthy. For too many years, I relied on myself. Then, God showed me that I could always depend on Him. I like this acronym:

F ully
R ely
O n
G od

Dear Father,

I want to completely trust and rely on you for everything in my life. I am counting on you to show me how to rely on YOU fully.

With love,

Me

_____
_____
_____
_____
_____
_____
_____
_____
_____
_____
_____
_____
_____
_____
_____
_____
_____
_____
_____
_____
_____
_____
_____

Faith Step: Whom have you relied on in the past? Other people? Yourself? Consider what steps of faith God is asking you to take today to learn how to rely on Him fully.

Day 3
Are you a Prisoner?

"Be kind and compassionate to one another, forgiving each other, just as in Christ God forgave you"
— *Ephesians 4:32 (NIV).*

Are you harboring a grudge? Angry with someone? Is bitterness holding you back from enjoying life? For years, I carried around bitterness and hurt. Until I learned to forgive, I was not free. I like this anonymous quote:

"When I forgave, I set a prisoner free. Then I realized the prisoner was me."

Dear Father,

I want to forgive those who have hurt me. I want to forgive myself for poor choices in the past. Please show me how to do this, Father.

With love,

Me

_____
_____
_____
_____
_____
_____
_____
_____
_____
_____
_____
_____
_____
_____
_____
_____
_____
_____
_____
_____
_____
_____
_____
_____
_____
_____
_____

Faith Step: Learn to forgive. Journal about those things that have led to your bitterness and anger. Now choose to forgive. Pour out your heart to the One who knows you better than you know yourself.

Day 4
Are you Afraid?

"For you did not receive a spirit that makes you a slave again to fear, but you received the Spirit of sonship. And by Him we cry, 'Abba, Father'"— Romans 8:15 (NIV).

As a child, I was afraid of the dark. I don't know why or when I outgrew my fear of things that go bump in the night. Fear can take us places we never intended to go. I like this acronym:

F alse
E vidence
A ppearing
R eal

Dear Father,

I am so afraid of things over which I have no control. Help me, Abba Father, to let go of my fears.

With love,

Me

_____
_____
_____
_____
_____
_____
_____
_____
_____
_____
_____
_____
_____
_____
_____
_____
_____
_____
_____
_____
_____
_____
_____
_____
_____

Faith Step: What are your fears? Write them out so you can face them. Ask your Abba Father to help you see that HE has not given you a spirit of fear.

Day 5
Down with Doubt!

"Fight the good fight of faith. Take hold of the eternal life . . ."—1 Timothy 6:12 (NIV).

According to the dictionary, doubt means to be uncertain about; consider questionable or unlikely; hesitate to believe; to distrust. Doubt can confuse and make you reconsider your faith.

Dear Father,

Sometimes I am confused. I don't want to be a doubting believer.
With love,

Me

_____
_____
_____
_____
_____
_____
_____
_____
_____
_____
_____
_____
_____
_____
_____
_____
_____
_____
_____
_____
_____
_____
_____
_____
_____
_____
_____
_____
_____
_____
_____
_____
_____
_____

Faith Step: Doubt has caused many people a great deal of pain. When you find yourself struggling, know that God has provided a way to overcome doubt. What are your doubts? Ask God to help you overcome them.

Day 6
Let Go of Your Anxiety

"Do not be anxious about anything, but in every situation, by prayer and petition, with thanksgiving, present your requests to God"— Philippians 4:6(NIV).

Every one of us spends too much time worrying about things that never materialize. Worry only makes our lives unnecessarily complicated and painful. However, there is hope. Your hope is found in God and God alone. Ford Motor Company founder, Henry Ford once said, "I believe God is managing affairs and that He doesn't need any advice from me. With God in charge, I believe everything will work out for the best in the end. So what is there to worry about?"

Dear Father,
Teach me, Father, to let go of those things over which I have no control.
With love,

Me

_____
_____
_____
_____
_____
_____
_____
_____
_____
_____
_____
_____
_____
_____
_____
_____
_____
_____
_____
_____
_____
_____
_____
_____
_____
_____
_____
_____
_____

Faith Step: In Matthew 6:25, Jesus says, "For this reason I say to you, do not be worried about your life, as to what you will eat or what you will drink; nor for your body, as to what you will put on. Is not life more than food and the body more than clothing?" Why worry? Make a list of your worries. Then, make a list of reasons not to be anxious about anything.

Day 7
Where's your Joy?

"I have come that they may have life, and have it to the full."—John 10:10 (NIV).

I can recall allowing others and my circumstances to steal my joy. While happiness can be found in external circumstances, no one can steal your joy unless you allow them to. I have learned that joy comes from having a relationship with my Heavenly Father and no one can ever take that away.

Dear Father,

Sometimes it is not easy to find joy during the tough times. I thank you, Father, that my joy is found in You.

With love,

Me

_____
_____
_____
_____
_____
_____
_____
_____
_____
_____
_____
_____
_____
_____
_____
_____
_____
_____
_____
_____
_____
_____
_____
_____
_____
_____
_____
_____

Faith Step: Psalm 126:3 says, "The Lord has done great things for us, and we are filled with joy." What great things has the Lord done for you? Thank Him and shout for joy!

Day 8
Live a Life of Love

"And now these three remain: faith, hope and love. But the greatest of these is love"
— *1 Corinthians 13:13(NIV).*

How do you learn to love others? Jesus tells us that we are to love our neighbors as ourselves. Sometimes, we find it difficult to love those who are unlovable. Ask God to let you see others through His eyes.

Dear Father,

Help me to cultivate the ability to love others, even those who are hard to love.

With love,

Me

_____
_____
_____
_____
_____
_____
_____
_____
_____
_____
_____
_____
_____
_____
_____
_____
_____
_____
_____
_____
_____
_____
_____
_____
_____
_____
_____
_____

Faith Step: Did you know that when you love others, your life is joy-filled? When your life is filled with love, you find a reason for living. What is your reason for living? Is it love?

Day 9
Cleanse Me Lord

*"If confess our sins, he is faithful and just and will forgive us our sins
and purify us from all unrighteousness"— 1 John 1:9 (NIV).*

I remember hearing someone say, "I haven't sinned in 10 years." I wanted to say, "You've just sinned by telling a falsehood." None of us is without sin. None but the Lamb of God is pure.

Dear Father,

I come humbly before you and ask you to cleanse my heart and renew a right spirit within me.

With love,

Me

_____
_____
_____
_____
_____
_____
_____
_____
_____
_____
_____
_____
_____
_____
_____
_____
_____
_____
_____
_____
_____
_____
_____
_____
_____
_____
_____
_____
_____
_____
_____

Faith Step: God is gracious and merciful, slow to anger and of great kindness (Joel 2:13). What sins do you need to confess? Ask God for forgiveness today.

Day 10
Walking in HIS Ways

"For just as through the disobedience of the one man the many were made sinners, so also through the obedience of the one man the many will be made righteous"— Romans 5:19(NIV).

Following Jesus is not easy. We cannot do it on our own. Being obedient to our Heavenly Father requires a daily dying to self. Adam and Eve disobeyed a simple command from God. Jesus, however, through His obedience on the cross, made us righteous.

Dear Father,

Please enable me to live in obedience to each part of Your law so that I might have peace.

With love,

Me

_____
_____
_____
_____
_____
_____
_____
_____
_____
_____
_____
_____
_____
_____
_____
_____
_____
_____
_____
_____
_____
_____
_____
_____
_____
_____
_____
_____

Faith Step: Study God's Word so you know how to live in obedience to Him. Ask Him to help you obey. Ask Him to show you were you are disobedient. Seek Him with all your heart, mind and soul.

Day 11
As a Man Thinketh

"'For my thoughts are not your thoughts, neither are your ways my ways,' declares the Lord"
— Isaiah 55:8 (NIV).

An earworm is a piece of music that sticks in one's mind so that one seems to hear it, even when it is not being played. What thoughts stick in your mind all day? Are they pleasant thoughts of God or troubling thoughts over which you have no control?

Dear Father,

I want my mind renewed by Your spirit, a spirit of righteousness and holiness.

With love,

Me

_____
_____
_____
_____
_____
_____
_____
_____
_____
_____
_____
_____
_____
_____
_____
_____
_____
_____
_____
_____
_____
_____
_____
_____
_____

Faith Step: As you read the Word, ask God to reveal any wrong thinking in you. Ask Him to renew your mind to release any foolish or futile thoughts. Thank Him that you "have the mind of Christ" (1 Corinthians 2:16).

Day 12
Who, or What, is Lord of Your Life?

"If we live, we live for the Lord; and if we die, we die for the Lord. So, whether we live or die, we belong to the Lord"— Romans 14:8 (NIV).

In Matthew 6:21, Jesus said, "For where your treasure is, there your heart will be also." Who or what is Lord of your life? Is it Jesus or do material things rule your life? I remember a time when having things and keeping up with other's expectations ruled my life. What about you? Are you living for the Lord?

Dear Father,

I love you with all my heart, with all my soul, and with all my mind. Teach me to deny myself in order to take up my cross daily and follow you.

With love,

Me

_____
_____
_____
_____
_____
_____
_____
_____
_____
_____
_____
_____
_____
_____
_____
_____
_____
_____
_____
_____
_____
_____
_____
_____
_____

Faith Step: Do you desire to please the Lord? Have you surrendered every part of your life to Him? Your body, your mind, your soul? Your relationships, your finances, your decisions and your desires? What is holding you back from surrendering all to Jesus?

Day 13
Have You Read the Best Seller?

"All Scripture is God-breathed and is useful for teaching, rebuking, correcting and training in righteousness"—2 Timothy 3:16(NIV).

Have you read the best-selling book of all time? I'm not talking about the latest thriller or romance. However, you can find many thrilling adventures and romances in the Bible. Did you know God loves you so much He gave His only Son so that you might have eternal life? Isn't that the best love story of all?

Dear Father,

I want to understand Your Word. Enable me to comprehend its deepest meaning.

With love,

Me

_____
_____
_____
_____
_____
_____
_____
_____
_____
_____
_____
_____
_____
_____
_____
_____
_____
_____
_____
_____
_____
_____
_____
_____
_____
_____
_____
_____
_____
_____

Faith Step: If you haven't read the Bible, what has kept you from studying God's Holy Word? Maybe you need to find a translation you can understand. Ask God to direct your path as you read His Word each day. He will. Don't let a lack of understanding keep you from reading the bestselling book of all time. "Your Word is a lamp unto my feet and a light to my path" (Psalm 119:105).

Day 14
Do it All in His Name!

*"And whatever you do, whether in word or deed, do it all in the name of the Lord Jesus,
giving thanks to God the Father through him"— Colossians 3:17(NIV).*

Have you ever been asked to do something you really didn't want to do? What was your response? Did you know you are blessed to be a blessing? Mother Teresa once said, "The miracle is not that we do this work, but that we are happy to do it."

Dear Father,

Help me to see others through Your gracious eyes. If I overlook someone's need, make me aware and show me how to be a blessing.

With love,

Me

_____
_____
_____
_____
_____
_____
_____
_____
_____
_____
_____
_____
_____
_____
_____
_____
_____
_____
_____
_____
_____
_____
_____
_____

Faith Step: When was the last time you sought out someone so you could be a blessing to them? How did you feel? Have you felt the Holy Spirit nudging you to reach out to someone? Did you follow through? Ask God to show you who needs your blessings today.

Day 15
Fix Your Eyes on Jesus

"Let us fix our eyes on Jesus, the author and perfecter of our faith, who for the joy set before him endured the cross, scorning its shame, and sat down at the right hand of the throne of God"
— Hebrews 12:2(NIV).

Where is your mind focused? Do you dwell on your weaknesses and failures? Do you dwell on your problems?

Dear Father,

I want to stay positive and focused on Jesus today. Please direct my thoughts and my path.
With love,

Me

_____
_____
_____
_____
_____
_____
_____
_____
_____
_____
_____
_____
_____
_____
_____
_____
_____
_____
_____
_____
_____
_____
_____
_____
_____
_____
_____

Faith Step: We all have weaknesses, failures and problems but Jesus has already overcome the world. Keep your "faith" focused on Jesus. Seek Him. Read His words in the Gospels. Keep following Him. Ask Jesus to help you stay positive and focused on Him today.

Day 16
You Are Blessed

"A faithful person will be richly blessed, but one eager to get rich will not go unpunished"
— Proverbs 28:20(NIV).

I love the following song lyrics: "Praise God from whom all blessings flow. Praise Him all creatures here below. Praise Him all of you Heavenly Hosts. Praise Father, Son and Holy Ghost." What comes to mind when you hear the word prosperity? Is money the first thing you envision? Most people equate being prosperous with finances. However, a constant flow of blessings is more precious than gold.

Dear Father,

Please help me to see my blessings today.

With love,

Me

_____
_____
_____
_____
_____
_____
_____
_____
_____
_____
_____
_____
_____
_____
_____
_____
_____
_____
_____
_____
_____
_____
_____
_____
_____
_____
_____
_____
_____
_____
_____

Faith Step: Today, count your blessings instead of your currency. Give thanks and praise to your Creator for the many blessings in your life. List your blessings. Thank Him!

Day 17
Muzzle my Mouth, Lord!

"Do not let any unwholesome talk come out of your mouths, but only what is helpful for building others up according to their needs, that it may benefit those who listen"— Ephesians 4:29 (NIV).

Until I accepted Jesus' invitation to be Lord of my life, I often let my tongue run loose. In other words, I put my mouth in gear before I engaged my brain. Proverbs 141:3 became my scripture until I learned to control my mouth:

"Set a guard over my mouth, O Lord; keep watch over the door of my lips."

Dear Father,

Please guide my thoughts and the words that leave my mouth today.
With love,

Me

_____
_____
_____
_____
_____
_____
_____
_____
_____
_____
_____
_____
_____
_____
_____
_____
_____
_____
_____
_____
_____
_____
_____
_____
_____
_____
_____
_____
_____

Faith Step: James mentions the tongue more than any other book in the Bible. If you have trouble controlling your tongue, locate those scriptures and write them down above. Ask God to help you keep a guard over the door of your lips.

Day 18
Are you Grumpy or Grateful?

"The word of Christ must live in you richly. Teach and warn each other with all wisdom by singing psalms, hymns, and spiritual songs. Sing to God with gratitude in your hearts"
— *Colossians 3:16(CEB).*

According to a 2010 "Wall Street Journal" story by Melinda Beck, "Adults who frequently feel grateful have more energy, more optimism, more social connections and more happiness than those who do not. They're also less likely to be depressed, envious, greedy or alcoholics. They earn more money, sleep more soundly, exercise more regularly, and have greater resistance to viral infections." Isn't that a good reason to be grateful instead of grumpy?

Dear Father,
Please forgive me when I am grumpy.
With love,
Me

_____

Faith Step: What are you grateful for today? Thank your Heavenly Father for your blessings. Sing a song of gratitude or compose a poem to Him.

Day 19
Putting Your Life in Order

"Whoever finds their life will lose it, and whoever loses their life for my sake will find it"
–Matthew 10:39 (NIV).

Are your priorities in line with God's will? Do you put Him first? Have you let Him put your life in order?

Dear Father,

Please help me to prioritize my life in a way that is pleasing in Your eyes.

With love,

Me

_____
_____
_____
_____
_____
_____
_____
_____
_____
_____
_____
_____
_____
_____
_____
_____
_____
_____
_____
_____
_____
_____
_____
_____
_____
_____
_____
_____
_____
_____
_____

Faith Step: What are your life's priorities? Do you spend time with Him, seeking His guidance before you start your busy day? Have you "lost" your life for His sake?

Day 20
Prayer is Good Medicine

"As for me, I said, 'O Lord, be gracious to me;
heal me, for I have sinned against you!'"— Psalm 41:4 (ESV).

Miracles can happen. I've experienced them. However, God doesn't always heal our physical bodies. Prayer does help us to trust God, who helps us to heal in the way that's best for us. He brings healing in many different ways: recovery, strength, closeness to Him, love, peace or support.

Dear Father,

I know you bring healing in many different ways. I thank you for your healing power in me today.

With love,

Me

Faith Step: Prayer helps us to feel less isolated when we or a loved one is ill. Not all illness, however, is physical. Some of our hurts cannot be seen but still cause us pain. Prayer can help us to let go of past hurts only God can see. Ask God to help you identify and heal past hurts.

Day 21
Are you Feasting?

"Jesus answered, 'It is written: Man shall not live on bread alone, but on every word that comes from the mouth of God'"—Matthew 4:4(NIV).

Scanning magazine cover headlines while standing in a grocery checkout line, can leave your brain addled. One magazine touts the benefits of eating a certain food while another headline reports that the same food is not beneficial to your health. Conflicting information leads to confusion. However, God's Holy Word, our Bread of Life, never changes.

Dear Father,

I want to feast on the only thing that satisfies me eternally. Please help me to understand Your Word.
With love,

Me

_____
_____
_____
_____
_____
_____
_____
_____
_____
_____
_____
_____
_____
_____
_____
_____
_____
_____
_____
_____
_____
_____
_____
_____
_____

Faith Step: If reading the Bible is not part of your routine, don't get overwhelmed thinking you have to read it like a novel. While the Bible is an interesting, exciting and suspenseful book, it's written for you to read, reread, meditate on and digest slowly. As you begin reading His Word, ask Him to reveal Himself to you. Trust me, He will.

Day 22
What's Holding you Back?

"The world is full of so-called prayer warriors who are prayer-ignorant.
They're full of formulas and programs and advice, peddling techniques for getting what you want from
God. Don't fall for that nonsense. This is your Father you are dealing with,
and He knows better than you what you need"—Matthew 6:7-8(MSG).

What's holding you back from being authentic with Your Heavenly Father? He already knows what you need before you even ask. We confuse our wants with our needs. He is a loving Father, who wants to hear your heartfelt thanks for what He had already done for you through the death of His precious Son on the cross.

Dear Father,

Please help me to search my heart honestly. Show me how to deal with the issues, both seen and unseen, that hold me back from being authentic with you.

With love,

Me

_____

_____

_____

_____

_____

_____

_____

_____

_____

_____

_____

_____

_____

_____

_____

_____

_____

_____

_____

_____

_____

_____

_____

Faith Step: In Matthew 6:9-13, Jesus taught His disciples how to pray. We can recite the Lord's Prayer in church, but have you examined it line-by-line in light of your own life? Use the space above to examine what God is trying to teach you about prayer.

Day 23
Have you met the Living Christ?

*"I have come into the world as a light, so that no one
who believes in me should stay in darkness"—John 12:46 (NIV).*

John 12:37 reveals "Even after Jesus had performed so many signs in their presence, they still would not believe in him." If we believe that Jesus is who He said He is, why do some still doubt Him? Although we are works-in-progress, we must remember that Jesus is our light. He is the Living Christ. He didn't stay on the cross, nor did He remain in the tomb. He's still alive and working in people's lives today.

Dear Father,

I believe in your Son. I believe He died and rose again. He is my light.

With love,

Me

_____
_____
_____
_____
_____
_____
_____
_____
_____
_____
_____
_____
_____
_____
_____
_____
_____
_____
_____
_____
_____
_____
_____
_____

Faith Step: If you have accepted Jesus as Your Savior, can you recall the first time you met the Living Christ? What was your spiritual life like when you first trusted Jesus? If you haven't accepted Jesus as Your Savior and wish to, pray the following prayer: "Lord Jesus, I believe you are the Son of God. Thank you for dying on the cross for my sins. Please forgive my sins and give me the gift of eternal life. I ask you into my life and heart to be my Lord and Savior. I want to serve you always."

Day 24
Experiencing His Presence

"You make known to me the path of life; you will fill me with joy in your presence, with eternal pleasures at your right hand"— Psalm 16:11(NIV).

Author and Pastor Henry Blackaby once said, "God is interested in developing your character. At times, He lets you proceed, but He will never let you go too far without discipline to bring you back. In your relationship with God, He may let you make a wrong decision. Then the Spirit of God causes you to recognize that it is not God's will. He guides you back to the right path." If we don't spend time in His presence, how can we know which way to go? However, if we make a mistake, He does allow u-turns.

Dear Father,

Thank you, Father, that I can experience Your presence and that You make known to me the path of life. Thank You that when I stray from Your path, You allow u-turns.

With love,

Me

_____
_____
_____
_____
_____
_____
_____
_____
_____
_____
_____
_____
_____
_____
_____
_____
_____
_____
_____
_____
_____
_____
_____
_____
_____
_____
_____

Faith Step: What has God done in your life or through your life that has caused you to experience His presence? Have you ever strayed from God? How did He draw you back onto the path He has for you?

Day 25
Walking in Obedience

"Observe the commands of the Lord your God, walking in obedience to him and revering him"— Deuteronomy 8:6 (NIV).

Many equate obedience with discipline. Schoolchildren know that if they don't follow the rules, they will be disciplined. When children disobey their parents, they have to accept the consequences. If we are caught speeding 55 in a 45, we may have to pay a fine, unless we get a warning from the officer. If we don't observe God's commands, we pay the price. Beginning with Adam and Eve, who disobeyed God's command to forgo eating the fruit from the Tree of Knowledge of Good and Evil, man has suffered the consequences of sin.

Dear Father,

I want to observe your commands. Please write your laws on my heart.

With love,

Me

Faith Step: What acts of obedience have you taken this week? What acts of obedience do you know God wants you to take? What will you do?

Day 26
Are you Thirsty?

"O God, you are my God; I earnestly search for you. My soul thirsts for you; my whole body longs for you in this parched and weary land where there is no water"— *Psalm 63:1(NLT).*

When I competed in 5K races, I had to stay hydrated if I wanted to do my best. Up to 60 percent of the human body is water. If we want to do more than survive, we need the Living Water to do our best. Jesus is the water that brings life to the soul. By drinking the living water, one can live and never thirst again. Jesus is that Living Water.

Dear Father,

I thirst for more of You, Jesus, the Living Water.

With love,

Me

_____
_____
_____
_____
_____
_____
_____
_____
_____
_____
_____
_____
_____
_____
_____
_____
_____
_____
_____
_____
_____
_____
_____
_____
_____
_____
_____
_____

Faith Step: Make a list of things you would like to learn about God. Ask Him to lead you to scriptures, books, study groups and seasoned Christians to help you learn more about His Son, the Living Water.

Day 27
Healing a Broken Heart

"Is anyone crying for help? God is listening, ready to rescue you. If your heart is broken, you'll find God right there; if you're kicked in the gut, he'll help you catch your breath"—*Psalm 34:17-18(MSG).*

Although I have scars on my body from eight surgeries and numerous childhood accidents, no one could see the traces of hurt leading to the wounds in my spirit—the ones that broke my heart. However, my *Abba Father* has brought healing. God's plan for us does not include living in the past. He wants us whole and healed—no matter what has happened in our lives.

Dear Father,

I know You want me to be whole. Please point out to me any area of my life of which I am unaware that needs healing.

With love,

Me

_____
_____
_____
_____
_____
_____
_____
_____
_____
_____
_____
_____
_____
_____
_____
_____
_____
_____
_____
_____
_____
_____
_____
_____
_____
_____

Faith Step: At the top of this page, write the word, "Pain." Underneath, make a list of any past hurts that have led to heartbreak. Don't hesitate, just write. Don't censor your thoughts. Select one to focus on, especially if your heart jumped when you wrote down a particular word. Ask God, "Where were You when this happened to me?" Reflect on how God might answer you.

Day 28
Are You Listening?

"'When I called, they did not listen,' says the Lord. 'So when they called, I would not listen'"— Zechariah 7:13 (NIRV).

According to the International Listening Association website, most of us are distracted, preoccupied or forgetful about 75 percent of the time we should be listening. The website also revealed we listen at 125-250 words per minute, but think at 1000-3000 words per minute. When you spend time with God, are you listening or doing all the talking? Author and speaker Joyce Meyer says, "Too often we spend all of our time seeking God for answers to our problems when what we should be doing is just seeking God."

Dear Father,

Forgive me when I talk too much in Your presence. Please help me to remember that I have two ears and one mouth.

With love,

Me

_____
_____
_____
_____
_____
_____
_____
_____
_____
_____
_____
_____
_____
_____
_____
_____
_____
_____
_____
_____
_____
_____
_____
_____

Faith Step: Writing in a prayer journal is one way to stay focused on your time with God. Today, don't request anything from Him. Ask Him to reveal Himself to you. Speak less; listen more. Seek His Face, not His handout.

Day 29
Two Most Important Things in Life

"Some people did accept him. They believed in His name. He gave them the right to become children of God"—John 1:12(NIRV).

Can you name the two most important things in life? If you answered, "Knowing God," and "Knowing who you are in Christ," you are right. Without knowing this, nothing else matters. You are here for a reason. Your life is not your own. You were bought with a price, the blood of our precious Savior, who came to serve humankind. When you realize that, you become aware of "Whose" you are and why you are here.

Dear Father,

I belong to you. Please guide me on the path of righteousness.
With love,

Me

_____

Faith Step: Find and copy the following scriptures to understand more about who you are in Christ. 1 John 3:3; Ephesians 1:6; John 15:14; Romans 8:17; 1 Corinthians 6:17; 1 Corinthians 6:19; 1 Corinthians 12:27; Ephesians 1:1; Colossians 1:14; Colossians 2:10; Romans 8:1; 2 Corinthians 5:17; Colossians 3:12; 2 Corinthians 1:21; 2 Timothy 1:7; 2 Corinthians 6:1; John 15:16; Ephesians 2:18; 1 Peter 2:5; 2 Peter 1:4; Philippians 2:13; James 1:5.

Day 30
How's Your Faith?

"But without faith it is impossible to please Him, for he who comes to God must believe that He is, and that He is a rewarder of those who diligently seek Him"— Hebrews 11:6(NKJV).

Over the last 10 years, I have taken many leaps of faith. According to "Wikipedia," a leap of faith, in its most commonly used meaning, "is the act of believing in or accepting something intangible or unprovable, or without empirical evidence." Many people need concrete evidence of God's existence. They don't trust what they can't see.

Dear Father,

I want to please you, Abba Father. I will diligently seek You each day.

With love,

Me

_____
_____
_____
_____
_____
_____
_____
_____
_____
_____
_____
_____
_____
_____
_____
_____
_____
_____
_____
_____
_____
_____
_____
_____
_____
_____
_____
_____

Faith Step: If you had perfect faith in God, what would you dare to do?

Day 31
A Good Work

"...being confident of this, that he who began a good work in you will carry it on to completion until the day of Christ Jesus"— Philippians 1:6(NIV).

Did you know that trials in life lead to your spiritual growth? When you accept Jesus as your Savior, it's only the first step in your journey to grow more like Him. He wants to take your relationship with Him to a new level. Your faith will grow and with each challenge you face, you will be strengthened.

Dear Father,

I know trials help me grow. Please give me strength and direction for my journey of trials.
With love,

Me

_____
_____
_____
_____
_____
_____
_____
_____
_____
_____
_____
_____
_____
_____
_____
_____
_____
_____
_____
_____
_____
_____
_____
_____
_____
_____
_____
_____
_____
_____
_____

Faith Step: When your trials seem overwhelming, remember Philippians 1:6 and ask God to provide strength and endurance. What trials have you overcome with His help? Are you facing any trials now? Thank Him for the trials He has already helped you conquer.

Day 32
Your Body is a Temple

"Or don't you know that your body is a temple of the Holy Spirit who is in you? Don't you know that you have the Holy Spirit from God, and you don't belong to yourselves? You have been bought and paid for, so honor God with your body"— 1 Corinthians 6:19-20 (CEB).

When some people read this scripture, they cringe. When we are not putting healthy things in our body, we grieve our Heavenly Father. When we realize our life is a gift from God then we should make the choice to take care of it by eating healthy, exercising on a regular basis and avoiding unhealthy habits, like smoking. It's not easy to give up unhealthy habits and adopt new ones.

Dear Father,

I want my life to honor you in every way. My body was purchased with the price of Your Son's blood. Give me the wisdom and strength to make the necessary changes for a healthy lifestyle.

With love,

Me

_____
_____
_____
_____
_____
_____
_____
_____
_____
_____
_____
_____
_____
_____
_____
_____
_____
_____
_____
_____
_____
_____
_____

Faith Step: It's not easy to give up unhealthy habits and adopt new ones. Adopt one new healthy habit each week. For example, start a walking routine of 10 minutes per day and gradually increase the time each week. Search for successful stories of others who have succeeded in losing weight and getting healthy for life. Let their success inspire you. If you need to quit smoking, see a doctor for help. Write down a plan above and ask God for His guidance.

Day 33
Refresh Your Spirit

"...that times of refreshing may come from the presence of the Lord" — Acts 3:19 (YLT).

Did you know the clearness of your mind and soul fades when you drift away from your Heavenly Father? However, when you surrender your life to God and seek His will in daily prayer, you are restored. We all need "times of refreshing" which can only come in the presence of the Lord. Life then becomes clean, fresh and enjoyable again.

Dear Father,

Please restore me in your Holy Presence and teach me to abide in You.

With love,

Me

_____
_____
_____
_____
_____
_____
_____
_____
_____
_____
_____
_____
_____
_____
_____
_____
_____
_____
_____
_____
_____
_____
_____
_____
_____
_____
_____
_____
_____
_____
_____

Faith Step: Have you drifted away from Your Heavenly Father? Seek the refreshment of His presence today. What can you do today to stay connected to Him?

Day 34
God's Door is always Open

"So in Christ Jesus you are all children of God through faith, for all of you who were baptized into Christ have clothed yourselves with Christ. There is neither Jew nor Gentile, neither slave nor free, nor is there male and female, for you are all one in Christ Jesus"— Galatians 3:26-28(NIV).

Have you ever felt left out in a group? Have you been places where you felt you didn't belong? I have. I can recall being invited to events but feeling so out-of-place I didn't want to stay. Since I have come to have a personal relationship with Jesus, I never feel left out.

Dear Father,
I know your door is always open to me. As your child, I belong everywhere. Thank you, Father.
With love,

Me

_____
_____
_____
_____
_____
_____
_____
_____
_____
_____
_____
_____
_____
_____
_____
_____
_____
_____
_____
_____
_____
_____
_____
_____

Faith Step: God's kingdom is open to those who accept Jesus. HIS door is never closed. Do you know people who feel out of place? What can you do to pass on God's acceptance and love to those who feel out-of-place?

Day 35
Be Open to Divine Appointments

"Do not boast about tomorrow, for you do not know what a day may bring"— *Proverbs 27:1 (NIV).*

I love it when God winks. Have you ever heard that expression? Squire Rushnell, author of *When God Winks*, says, "A godwink is what some people would call a coincidence, an answered prayer, or simply an experience where you'd say, 'Wow, what are the odds of that!'" I think we have to be open to God's divine appointments each day, which means we shouldn't hold too tight to our own plans.

Dear Father,

Please help me to be flexible when the unexpected enters my day and to look for Your winks.
With love,

Me

_____
_____
_____
_____
_____
_____
_____
_____
_____
_____
_____
_____
_____
_____
_____
_____
_____
_____
_____
_____
_____
_____
_____
_____
_____
_____
_____
_____

Faith Step: We don't know what we will encounter each day. We can make plans but must learn to be flexible and open to God's winks. Can you recall any He has sent your way? What happened? Look at each person today as someone God has sent into your life.

Day 36
This is the Way

"Whether you turn to the right or to the left, your ears will hear a voice behind you, saying, 'This is the way; walk in it'"— Isaiah 30:21 (NIV).

How do you know what God wants you to do with your life? Do you know how to make decisions that honor Him? Wouldn't it be nice if He would just send an email or postcard each morning with specific instructions for the next step you need to take? He doesn't; however, He does offer guidance through His Word and godly people we have learned to trust.

Dear Father,

I am seeking Your wisdom today. I trust that You will guide me because You want me to walk in Your ways.
With love,

Me

_____

Faith Step: Step out in faith today, knowing that God will direct your steps. If you're trying to make a major decision about a life change, write down each option and the pros and cons of each. Have you made a major change in your life before? What did you do before that change? Did you seek God's wisdom? Why or why not? Will you do so in the future?

Day 37
Laugh Out Loud & On Purpose

"A cheerful disposition is good for your health;
gloom and doom leave you bone-tired"—Proverbs 17:22(MSG).

Do you spend your days fretting over the news, asking yourself, "What if?" If so, you might just be bone-tired of the gloom and doom headlines. Negativity can rob us of our joy. What's a good solution? Get away from the TV news and the newspaper headlines and spend some time with those you love. I love spending time outdoors with my grandchildren. Their antics keep my insides exercised with laughter. It's good for your health and your soul.

Dear Father,
Sometimes I become overwhelmed and bone-tired of all the bad news in today's world.
With love,

Me

_____
_____
_____
_____
_____
_____
_____
_____
_____
_____
_____
_____
_____
_____
_____
_____
_____
_____
_____
_____
_____
_____
_____
_____
_____
_____
_____

Faith Step: When was the last time you had a good belly laugh? What was the situation? With whom did you share laughter? Make it a point to find something to laugh about each day.

Day 38
Share the Load

"For my yoke is easy, and my burden is light"—Matthew 11:30(ESV).

Around the age of two, children start seeking some independence. My youngest grandson doesn't want assistance putting on his clothes, saying, "I can do it myself, Nana." Just like a two-year-old, we sometimes tell God, "I can do it myself." Our stubborn pride won't let us admit that we need His help or anyone else's assistance. I've been there, done that, and still struggle with allowing people to help me.

Dear Father,

Forgive me when my pride prevents me from asking for Your help.

With love,

Me

_____
_____
_____
_____
_____
_____
_____
_____
_____
_____
_____
_____
_____
_____
_____
_____
_____
_____
_____
_____
_____
_____
_____
_____
_____
_____
_____
_____
_____
_____
_____

Faith Step: You don't need to carry your burdens without assistance. God wants to help you carry them. What difficulties have you been trying to carry alone? Share the load with your loving Savior.

Day 39
Lost and Found

"Give and it will be given to you. A good measure, pressed down, shaken together and running over, will be poured into your lap. For with the measure you use, it will be measured to you"
—*Luke 6:38(NIV).*

If you're lost, the only way to find yourself is to lose yourself in things outside yourself. Sound confusing. Here's the simplified version: The more you give, the more you receive from life.

Dear Father,

I'm lost. Please help me to be open to others and their needs.

With love,

Me

_____
_____
_____
_____
_____
_____
_____
_____
_____
_____
_____
_____
_____
_____
_____
_____
_____
_____
_____
_____
_____
_____
_____
_____
_____
_____
_____
_____
_____
_____
_____

Faith Step: Examine your life by asking the following question: "How can I give more than I receive?"

You can't outgive God, but you are blessed to be a blessing to others. Who needs a blessing today? Be creative. Think outside the box. What do you have in your possession that you could give away to someone who really needs it or would love to have it?

Day 40
Everything Changes—Except Jesus

"Jesus Christ is the same yesterday, today, and forever"—Hebrews 13:8(NIV).

Have you heard this quote? "You can't change a man unless he's in diapers." This also applies to women. Most people don't like change. It not only upsets their routine but there is fear of the unknown. We don't have to fear today or tomorrow because Jesus never changes. Everything around us will continue to change. We can't stop progress, nor can we change other people. The best change, however, is when we allow Jesus to do an extreme makeover on us, from the inside out.

Dear Father,

While I'm not afraid of change, I don't know where to start. Please guide me as I continue my journey, trusting Your Son to reveal what changes need to be made in me and in my life so that I am completely in Your will.

With love,

Me

_____
_____
_____
_____
_____
_____
_____
_____
_____
_____
_____
_____
_____
_____
_____
_____
_____
_____
_____
_____
_____
_____
_____
_____

Faith Step: Don't let your journey end here. Forty days is only the beginning of an exciting adventure with your Savior. He wants more for your life. He wants to help you continue the transformation so you can help Him in the process of changing the lives of other people. Are you ready? If Jesus were sitting across the breakfast table from you this morning, what would you ask Him?

Continuing Your Journey

"For I know the plans I have for you," declares the Lord, "plans to prosper you and not to harm you, plans to give you hope and a future"—Jeremiah 29:11 (NIV).

As you continue your journey to draw closer to your *Abba Father*, seek Him each morning with all your heart, with all your soul and all your mind. Read scriptures. Find a devotional that appeals to you and prepare for a lifetime of adventure with Jesus.

Keep on Journaling

Keep on Journaling

Keep on Journaling

Keep on Journaling

Keep on Journaling

Keep on Journaling

Keep on Journaling

Keep on Journaling

Keep on Journaling

About the Author

If someone were to ask me why I write, I would have to reply, "Why not?" It is part of who I am. As a child, my love of a good story often got me into trouble at school. I would hide my library book, usually a mystery, behind the pages of a bulky school text. That is probably the reason my grades suffered in other areas, especially math.

At night, my mother would often find me hiding under the bed sheets reading. This was after she had told me more than once to turn out the lights and go to sleep. I focused on the page with the help of a flashlight I had pilfered from Dad. As with most avid readers, I love the written word. I had dreams of being a famous writer one day, cut off from civilization, living life like Thoreau. I had no trouble, even as a child, imagining what it would be like to live on Walden Pond.

Because of my fascination with nature, my first attempts at writing were about God's divine creation. I wrote rhyming poems to express my love for everything outdoors: the spring flowers, the fall colors, dancing snowflakes and summer showers. I cringe now at my early endeavors because although I very seldom write poetry today, I prefer free verse.

For me, writing has become more than just playing with words. During times of trouble in my life, the written word has served as a catharsis. Keeping a journal, writing letters to God or making a list of goals has helped me to regroup, refocus and redefine my life.

After taking a six-week fiction-writing course at a community college, I completed ten chapters of a romantic suspense novel. Even though the writing instructor said I had a talent for that genre, I could never finish the book. I was going through a rough time in my life—separation and eventually a divorce. Only after this painful experience did I come to realize what was missing in my life. I grew up in the church. I believed in God. I knew of Him, but I didn't know Him.

As my relationship with the Lord has grown, so has my writing. Knowing Him has opened my heart, my eyes and my ears to a deeper understanding of life. With a wisdom born from failure and forgiveness, I have committed my writing to His glory.

At my core, I am a woman seeking more of Him and His will for my life. I hope one day to hear those wonderful words, *"Well done, my good and faithful servant."*

To My Readers

Did you finish the 40-day challenge? Congratulations! If you plan to continue "Journaling with Jesus," please contact me and let me know if keeping a prayer journal has changed your relationship with our Savior. Whether you continue to journal or not after the 40 days, I would still love to hear your feedback. You may contact me via email at **carolaround@yahoo.com**.

Also, please feel free to connect with me at:

- Blog:
  www.carolaround.com
- Book website:
  www.journalingwithjesus.com
- Facebook page:
  http://www.facebook.com/carolaround *(Please be sure and "friend" me.)*
- Facebook fan page:
  http://www.facebook.com/JournalingwithJesus *(Please be sure and "like" my page.)*
- My other Facebook fan page:
  http://www.facebook.com/pages/A-Matter-of-Faith/132121790200971
  (Please be sure and "like" my page.)
- Twitter:
  http://twitter.com/carolaround
- Utube:
  http://www.youtube.com/watch?v=0SJDd1L5VFs:
  Journaling with Jesus: How to Draw Closer to God book trailer
  (Would you please click "like," if you like it, and share it with your friends?)
- My Amazon.com author page:
  http://www.amazon.com/Carol-Round/e/B0083ZEAWI/ref=sr_ntt_srch_lnk_1?qid=1342565567&sr=1-1

If you haven't purchased a copy of my book, *Journaling with Jesus: How to Draw Closer to God,"* it is available at **www.amazon.com** as well as my website and blog. (See links above.)

What others are saying about

Journaling with Jesus: How to Draw Closer to God

"**This is a great book** to help anyone get started journaling in their spiritual life. Carol motivated me to be more disciplined in my prayer life. I actually started the book and couldn't put it down. I loved this book. If you are interested in journaling, you must read."   —Shellie Rhine, *Amazon review*

"Journaling is an age-old practice of examining one's life. It is a tremendous tool to track and measure learning, growth, and change. It can make a dramatic difference, especially when Jesus is invited into the process. That is what this book is all about. **I highly recommend** you get Carol's book and allow her journaling process to assist, enhance, and inspire yours."   —Nancy Slocum, *Amazon review*

"Allow *Journaling with Jesus* to take you deep into the heart of God, by showing you practically and inspirationally how to bare the depths of your own heart on the blank page. As you fill your journal with words of honesty, God will fill your heart with the wonder of His love."

—Lynn D. Morrissey, author
Love Letters to God: Deeper Intimacy through Written Prayer, speaker, journal facilitator

---

"Blessed to know that this little but very deep and **wonderful book points straight to God and His Words** as our basis to start with daily prayer journaling and to learn to understand them, which helps us understand God and His ways."   —Karen Lyons, *LyonsLady blog*

"Do you desire to have a more intimate relationship with the Lord? Are you unsure about how to achieve it? Carol Round's book will inspire, encourage, and—perhaps perhaps best of all—give you practical guidance on how to develop a closer walk and open up the lines of communication between you and God through journaling. Whether or not/however you journal, **this book will help you 'amp up' your prayer life**. Clearly, succinctly, and honestly written, you will find it helpful on a number of levels."

—Paula Smith, *Amazon review*

"Writing your thoughts and prayers to the Lord is a wonderful way to stay close to Him and also record the answers to your prayers. **I was so impressed with the book that I bought several to give** to my journaling children and grandchildren. Thank you, Carol Round, for a wonderful book!"

—Linda Huey, *Amazon review*

Made in the USA
Monee, IL
01 December 2020